SMALL STEPS. BIG IMPACT.

A Year of Simple Actions to Transform Your Life

Lanette Pottle

Copyright © 2018 Lanette Pottle

All rights reserved. This book or any portion thereof may not be reproduced or used in any manner whatsoever without the express written permission of the publisher except for the use of brief quotations in a book review.

Library of Congress Control Number: 2018911102

ISBN: 978-1-7327858-0-9

Book edited by Laurel Robinson
Book design by AHD Design

First printing, 2018.

Positivity Lady Press
1088 US Rte 1
Robbinston, ME 04671

www.positivityladypress.com

This book is dedicated with love and gratitude to my mentors.

Linda Godfrey, for asking the question that helped
me step into my purpose.

Jack Canfield, for sharing the knowledge and tools
that changed the trajectory of my life.

Gahmya Drummond-Bey, for inspiring me to think bigger
and nudging me to finally publish this book.

"When big feels overwhelming, start small."

LANETTE POTTLE

SIMPLE.
DELIBERATE.
CONSISTENT.
ACTION.

These four words capture the essence of the year-long adventure you are about to embark upon. The journey of transformation and making a difference in the world doesn't require a huge time commitment or a complicated plan. Too often we are paralyzed by the thought that transforming our lives means we must undertake projects on a grand scale. Nothing could be further from the truth. The pages that follow are a guide that will yield undeniable evidence of the power of small steps in creating positive changes in you and the world around you.

This work is based on two seemingly contradictory truths:

TRUTH 1:
The only person we can change is ourselves.

TRUTH 2:
Anyone (and everyone) can change the world. As you undertake each weekly activity, it is the intention behind your action that will make all the difference. When you act with an open, loving heart and a genuine desire to make positive changes, you can't help but be touched by the experience. And when you are changed, it affects others. This is the compounding effect that, over time, ultimately creates transformation.

As you prepare for this journey, here are five things you should keep in mind:

1. This guide has been developed as an interactive tool fueled by action. It's not meant to be read from cover to cover and then tucked away.

2. Consistency is the secret to transformation. It's not what you do occasionally that creates lasting change; it's what you do regularly.

3. If you are tempted to skip an activity because you have done it before, rethink your decision. Trust in the cumulative effect of repeating and building upon simple actions.

4. If you reach an activity that feels outside your comfort zone and you think you simply can't do it ... lean in and do it anyway. There are big rewards on the other side of your fear or limiting beliefs. The changes you make will be amplified.

5. Simple does not always mean easy.

As you embrace this journey and embark on adventures in positive action, I would love to hear about your experiences. Please send your stories to lanette@positivitylady.com.

Cheers to your success,

Lanette

PS: If you want to enhance your journey, I invite you to join me inside my private group, Positivity Nation. We are a community of change agents, difference makers, and positivity ignitors. Our focus is on supporting each other through brainstorming, problem solving, resource and idea sharing, and encouragement. You can find us at https://www.facebook.com/groups/positivitynation/.

WEEK 1

SAY THANK YOU

Mail a thank-you card or letter to someone who has been a positive influence in your life. Let them know how much their words and actions have meant to you.

Details About This Activity I Want To Remember:

WEEK 2

ACT RANDOMLY

ACT RANDOMLY

Deliver a random act of kindness. Do something nice for a stranger or someone you don't know very well. Take note of the reaction you get and how it makes you feel.

Details About This Activity I Want To Remember:

WEEK 3

BE GRATEFUL

Start a gratitude journal. Every day take time to record three things that you are thankful for. Stretch to include the less-than-pleasant things that may have helped you learn and grow.

Details About This Activity I Want To Remember:

WEEK 4

VISIT AN ELDER

VISIT AN ELDER

Visit an elderly neighbor or go to a nursing home. Engage in conversation, share a meal, play a game, help with a chore, or listen to a story and be genuinely interested.

Details About This Activity I Want To Remember:

"Gratitude makes sense of our past, brings peace for today, and creates a vision for tomorrow."

MELODY BEATTIE

> "We can only be said to be alive in the moments when our hearts are conscious of our treasures."
>
> **THORNTON WILDER**

WEEK 5

GET YOUR HANDS DIRTY

Reveal and revitalize the beauty in your neighborhood. Help in a community garden, lead a cleanup project, spruce up a park or Little League field.

Details About This Activity I Want To Remember:

WEEK 6: STOP COMPLAINING

Instead of complaining, look for solutions. Find a way to reframe your comments and thoughts. Keep track of your progress for the week and notice any recurring themes among the things you're tempted to complain about.

Details About This Activity I Want To Remember:

WEEK 7

ENCOURAGE A CHILD

Taking the time to encourage a child is a strong investment in the future. You may never know how important it is to them, but act anyway.

Details About This Activity I Want To Remember:

HELP THE HUNGRY

Donate to your local soup kitchen or food pantry. If a donation of goods or money is not something you can work into your budget, consider offering the priceless gift of your time.

Details About This Activity I Want To Remember:

> "Sometimes it's the smallest decisions that can change your life forever."
>
> **KERI RUSSELL**

"Do your little bit of good where you are. It's those little bits of good together that overwhelm the world."

DESMOND TUTU

WEEK 9

SUPPORT FURRY FRIENDS

There is always something that needs to be done at a local shelter! Provide a foster home for animals waiting to be placed. Donate food, blankets, cleaning supplies, or other frequently used items. Support fundraising events. Choose something and do it.

Details About This Activity I Want To Remember:

WEEK 10
SAVE YOUR CHANGE

Set aside your loose change each week and at the end of the year donate it to an organization doing good in your neighborhood. This is a financial contribution you can make without even feeling a pinch in your wallet!

Details About This Activity I Want To Remember:

DATE COMPLETED

WEEK 11

CLEAR THE CLUTTER

The key to decluttering your office, your files, your closet, or your car, is getting started. Make this the week you do, and notice how it clears the clutter in your mind, too.

Details About This Activity I Want To Remember:

DATE COMPLETED

WEEK 12

SHOP POSITIVELY

Support a business that supports others. Whether a portion of the proceeds is donated to a great cause, the product itself brings attention to an important issue, or the sale highlights fair-trade practices, how and where you spend your money makes a difference.

Details About This Activity I Want To Remember:

DATE COMPLETED

"Do what you can,
with what you have,
where you are."

THEODORE ROOSEVELT

"I am only one, but I am one. I cannot do everything, but I can do something. I will not let what I cannot do interfere with what I can do."

EDWARD EVERETT HALE

WEEK 13

HONOR A TEACHER

Honor that special person by volunteering at one of your local schools, donating to a charity or cause in their name, or maybe even taking them out to lunch! Keep in mind those on your journey who taught you lessons outside the classroom, too.

Details About This Activity I Want To Remember:

DATE COMPLETED

WEEK 14

SHARE APPRECIATION

Who is someone whose actions you might normally take for granted—the waitress who remembers your special preferences, the coworker whose smile brightens your day, the person who shares a joke at just the right time, or a friend who cares enough to share difficult feedback? Show people that you notice and that you appreciate them!

Details About This Activity I Want To Remember:

DATE COMPLETED

WEEK 15

LIFT YOUR VOICE

Be a catalyst for change. Call, write, visit, e-mail, or text an elected official (or a decision maker) about an issue that you are passionate about. Your voice matters.

Details About This Activity I Want To Remember:

DATE COMPLETED

WEEK 16

SPREAD GOOD NEWS

SPREAD GOOD NEWS

Make a deliberate effort to find positive news stories—then share them! Post them on your social media channels, share them with your coworkers, and tell your family—then ask them to do the same.

Details About This Activity I Want To Remember:

DATE COMPLETED

"Act as if what you do makes a difference. It does."

WILLIAM JAMES

"Inaction breeds doubt and fear. Action breeds confidence and courage. If you want to conquer fear, do not sit home and think about it. Go out and get busy."

DALE CARNEGIE

WEEK 17

EAT TOGETHER

Have at least one family dinner this week. Too often we get caught up in the business of life and forget the simple yet important ritual of sitting down together around the kitchen table. It doesn't have to be a fancy meal—the focus isn't the food, it's your family. Engage in conversation and use this time to reconnect with those you love.

Details About This Activity I Want To Remember:

DATE COMPLETED

WEEK 18

SAVE A LIFE

SAVE A LIFE

Sign an organ donor card, donate blood, register for a CPR or first aid course, or join the bone marrow registry. Maybe you'd like to volunteer for a crisis hotline, donate your time and talents to a shelter for abused women, or support an anti-bullying / pro-kindness campaign. This is your opportunity to be a real lifesaver.

Details About This Activity I Want To Remember:

DATE COMPLETED

WEEK 19

HAVE NO REGRETS

Leave no room for the would-haves, could-haves, should-haves, and what-ifs by making a little time this week for those you care about but haven't made a priority lately.

Details About This Activity I Want To Remember:

DATE COMPLETED

WEEK 20

LAUGH OUT LOUD

Laugh out loud ... and be sure it's not just a chuckle, but a from-the-pit-of-your-soul belly laugh! Make it your mission this week to watch a comedy, spend time with your funniest friend, or just look for the humor in every situation. A good dose of laughter can lift the grayest of spirits, energize you, and relieve stress.

Details About This Activity I Want To Remember:

DATE COMPLETED

"When we give cheerfully and accept gratefully, everyone is blessed."

MAYA ANGELOU

"You will discover that you have two hands. One is for helping yourself and the other is for helping others."

AUDREY HEPBURN

WEEK 21

PAY IT FORWARD

In recognition of those who have helped you along your path, take time this week to pass on their kindness by helping someone else in a similar way.

Details About This Activity I Want To Remember:

DATE COMPLETED

WEEK 22
SPEAK YOUR DREAM

Give voice to your life visions and dreams. Selectively share them with like-minded people who can help support, nurture, and encourage you as you begin to take action.

Details About This Activity I Want To Remember:

DATE COMPLETED

WEEK 23

READ TO A CHILD

Expand a child's imagination and fuel a love of reading. Revisit the fun of reading out loud, and enjoy the delight and wonder you will see in that child's eyes!

Details About This Activity I Want To Remember:

DATE COMPLETED

WEEK 24

GIVE A HUG

GIVE A HUG

Never underestimate the power of human touch. Whether you give it to your kids, your parents, a sibling, a friend, or someone who seems to be going through a tough time, this small gesture creates connection and could really turn someone's day around.

Details About This Activity I Want To Remember:

DATE COMPLETED

"One person can make a difference and everyone should try."

JOHN F. KENNEDY

" Kind words can be short and easy to speak but their echoes are truly endless."

MOTHER TERESA

WEEK 25

CREATE A PLAN

How are you going to make a positive difference at home, at your workplace, in your community, and in your circle of influence? Be specific. Be deliberate. Be courageous! Write it down on paper, so you can revisit your commitments and then record your results in your journal.

Details About This Activity I Want To Remember:

DATE COMPLETED

WEEK 26

HONOR A LIFE

There is no denying that the loss of a loved one is a painful experience. This week, dig deep to find a way to honor the life of that special person while also helping others. What hobby did this person love? What causes were they passionate about? What was your loved one best known for? Find a way to incorporate these things into giving acts.

Details About This Activity I Want To Remember:

DATE COMPLETED

WEEK 27

DO SOME WEEDING

Get rid of at least one negative thing from your life. This week, do a personal inventory, determine who or what is dragging you down, and make a change! Life is like gardening: you need to consistently pluck out the weeds so the sun can shine through. Make your garden beautiful this week!

Details About This Activity I Want To Remember:

DATE COMPLETED

WEEK 28

BECOME A CONDUIT

What introductions to people, products, and resources can you make—to acquaintances, colleagues, and friends—that will benefit them? Become known for your generosity of sharing in a way that supports others.

Details About This Activity I Want To Remember:

DATE COMPLETED

"When you change the way you look at things, the things you look at change."

WAYNE DYER

"You cannot change reality, but you can control the manner in which you look at things. Your attitude is under your control."

HELEN STEINER RICE

WEEK 29

BE STILL

In the hustle and bustle of life, we too often forget to just take a moment to be still, breathe, and be alone to connect with our thoughts. Practice this every day this week ... Start with just 60 quiet seconds, three times a day, and work your way up from there. Stick with it, and you'll start to feel your stress levels diminish.

Details About This Activity I Want To Remember:

DATE COMPLETED

WEEK 30

MAKE A LIST

Set aside time this week to begin creating a list of at least 100 things you love about yourself and your life. You may not finish this exercise in one sitting, or even in one week, but keep at it! Once you complete the list, tuck it away somewhere safe. When you encounter difficulties or experience a day when you are not feeling good about yourself, pull out your list. Reading through it will help put things into perspective and give you an emotional boost.

Details About This Activity I Want To Remember:

DATE COMPLETED

WEEK 31

FORGIVE YOURSELF

Forgive yourself for your past mistakes and shortcomings. Nothing good comes out of dwelling on what you cannot change. Extend yourself some grace. Let it go and release the hold your past has over you.

Details About This Activity I Want To Remember:

DATE COMPLETED

WEEK 32

ENJOY A DETOUR

ENJOY A DETOUR

Many times we are so focused on our "destination" that we don't take time to enjoy all the things we encounter on the journey. Whether you're on a road trip or concentrating on reaching a goal, remain aware of and open to all the wonderful things that cross your path. You may find that the detour is more spectacular than the destination!

Details About This Activity I Want To Remember:

DATE COMPLETED

"You cannot travel back in time to fix your mistakes, but you can learn from them and forgive yourself for not knowing better."

LES BROWN

"Love yourself, accept yourself, forgive yourself, and be good to yourself because without you the rest of us are without the source of many wonderful things."

LEO BUSCAGLIA

WEEK 33

BE A CHEERLEADER

Nothing is better than the energy you receive through the encouragement from a friend—or total stranger—cheering you on toward a milestone or goal. This week, be the giver of that energy.

Details About This Activity I Want To Remember:

DATE COMPLETED

WEEK 34

SAY NO

SAY NO

Don't get so busy with what everyone else thinks you should be doing that you lose sight of what is important to you! You will be the most effective when you are living authentically, listening to your inner voice, and acting to create the outcomes you desire. Sometimes that means saying no.

Details About This Activity I Want To Remember:

DATE COMPLETED

WEEK 35

BREATHE FRESH AIR

One of the best ways to rejuvenate is to get out into nature and just breathe it in. Take advantage of this natural resource, which is available to you free of charge.

Details About This Activity I Want To Remember:

DATE COMPLETED

WEEK 36

TELL THE BOSS

TELL THE BOSS

Take time this week to jot a note or make a phone call to the owner or manager of an establishment you frequent. Let them know what a great job your favorite employee is doing. Don't assume they know about the great service being provided ... Take the extra step and be sure the right person knows!

Details About This Activity I Want To Remember:

DATE COMPLETED

"It makes a big difference in your life when you stay positive."

ELLEN DEGENERES

"Joy comes to us in ordinary moments. We risk missing out when we get too busy chasing down extraordinary."

BRENÉ BROWN

WEEK 37

CHANGE YOUR PASSWORD

Practice positive self-talk in the most routine of ways! Develop passwords that give you a daily boost and make you feel good. Here are a few ideas to get you started: BNice2d@y, smileW!DE, IMW0rthy, 1AwesomeD@y, URamazing2.

Details About This Activity I Want To Remember:

DATE COMPLETED

WEEK 38

DELEGATE

DELEGATE

Just because you can do something doesn't mean it's yours to do. Make space in your schedule to do the things in your zone of genius by sharing responsibilities with others.

Details About This Activity I Want To Remember:

DATE COMPLETED

WEEK 39

TOSS SOME PRAISE

Throw out some praise with your rubbish! Surprise your trash collector with a cheery note of thanks. It will surely go a long way toward making his or her day.

Details About This Activity I Want To Remember:

DATE COMPLETED

WEEK 40

SAY I LOVE YOU

SAY I LOVE YOU

It's a simple thing that we too often overlook. Be sure that the people you care about know how you feel. Tell them today ... and often. Hearing that someone loves you never gets old!

Details About This Activity I Want To Remember:

DATE COMPLETED

> "Never confuse small with insignificant."
>
> — LANETTE POTTLE

"Be faithful in small things because it is in them that your strength lies."

MOTHER TERESA

WEEK 41

FIND BEAUTY

Peel back the layers, and look beneath the surface. Beauty is all around us ... even on the darkest days. We just need to be open and willing to see what is there.

Details About This Activity I Want To Remember:

DATE COMPLETED

WEEK 42

POST IT

POST IT

This week, pick up a pad of those little sticky notes and begin writing uplifting, inspiring, affirming, and empowering statements. When you are finished, post some around your house where you will see them often. Then spread the power of these little gems by posting them on mirrors and surfaces in public areas for others to see.

Details About This Activity I Want To Remember:

DATE COMPLETED

WEEK 43

INVEST IN YOURSELF

Whether it's enrolling in a class, attending a seminar, purchasing a suit that makes you feel like a million bucks, or something else that increases your knowledge or self-esteem, the return on your investment will be significant, and the risks will be minimal.

Details About This Activity I Want To Remember:

DATE COMPLETED

WEEK 44

SHARE YOUR STORY

When you share the obstacles and challenges you've overcome, it not only helps you recognize how far you've come, but inspires and empowers others to rise above their challenges, too.

Details About This Activity I Want To Remember:

DATE COMPLETED

"Doing the best at this moment puts you in the best place for the next moment."

OPRAH WINFREY

"Accept responsibility for your life. Know that it is you who will get you where you want to go, no one else."

LES BROWN

WEEK 45

TRY AGAIN

What is one thing that you really wanted to do but didn't succeed at in your first attempt? Just because it didn't work out then doesn't mean it won't now. Exercise your courage and try again!

Details About This Activity I Want To Remember:

DATE COMPLETED

WEEK 46
ELIMINATE INCOMPLETES

ELIMINATE INCOMPLETES

What projects have you started but not quite finished? Which relationships need closure? What difficult decisions do you keep delaying? Give these things priority attention this week.

Details About This Activity I Want To Remember:

DATE COMPLETED

WEEK 47

SHARE YOUR EXPERTISE

Sharing your knowledge can help someone grow, and the bonus is that we always learn when we teach. Your expertise may range from preparing nutritious meals on a budget to creating a marketing plan, from knitting mittens to financial planning, from making an incredible piecrust to fund raising, from developing the perfect foul shot to composting … The point is that we are all good at something!

Details About This Activity I Want To Remember:

DATE COMPLETED

WEEK 48

SEEK HARMONY

SEEK HARMONY

Make a conscious decision about how you spend your time. In addition to work, decide how you will include the activities that bring you joy. Your choices create your reality. Life is never perfectly balanced, but you have the power to create harmony through your deliberate actions.

Details About This Activity I Want To Remember:

DATE COMPLETED

> "It always seems impossible until it is done."
>
> **NELSON MANDELA**

"We gain strength, courage, and confidence by each experience in which we really stop to look fear in the face... we must do that which we think we cannot."

ELEANOR ROOSEVELT

WEEK 49

APOLOGIZE SINCERELY

You may not have intended to hurt someone's feelings, but you did. Take the time to acknowledge your shortcoming, and then apologize in a heartfelt, sincere manner and ask for forgiveness.

Details About This Activity I Want To Remember:

DATE COMPLETED

WEEK 50

BREAK THE CHAINS

BREAK THE CHAINS

We get used to our habits and routines and often become bound by our self-imposed limitations. This week, take a step outside your comfort zone and do something unexpected. Consider trying a new food or recipe. Make time to experience an adventure. Travel to someplace unfamiliar. Develop a new skill. Let your imagination guide you, and do something outside your "norm."

Details About This Activity I Want To Remember:

DATE COMPLETED

WEEK 51

TRUST YOURSELF

Lean in, listen to your intuition, and then follow through. Have you sometimes shown bad judgment? Who hasn't?! Chances are, it happened when you didn't listen to your intuition. You might not believe it, but somewhere deep inside, you really do have the answers … You only need to tune in and listen up.

Details About This Activity I Want To Remember:

DATE COMPLETED

WEEK 52

REFLECT

REFLECT

After spending this last year focusing on positive action, how has your life been transformed? Whose life have you influenced? Share your experiences with others and keep going. Continue to make your world better every day.

Details About This Activity I Want To Remember:

DATE COMPLETED

"Success is the sum of small efforts repeated day in and day out."

ROBERT COLLIER

"It is our own thoughts that hold the key to miraculous transformation."

MARIANNE WILLIAMSON

9 781732 785809